JAPAN AND THE
UNITED STATES IN ASIA

Studies in International Affairs Number 8

Studies in International Affairs Number 8

JAPAN AND THE UNITED STATES IN ASIA

by Robert E. Osgood, George R. Packard III, and John H. Badgley

The Washington Center of Foreign Policy Research
School of Advanced International Studies
The Johns Hopkins University

The Johns Hopkins Press, Baltimore

FOREWORD

More than twenty years after the defeat of Japan, America's former adversary in the Asian-Pacific area is its major ally. At the same time, despite previous military dominance and present industrial-technological pre-eminence, Japan remains quiescent under American protection. The first circumstance is analogous to other notable shifts of alignment in the history of international politics, but the second is something of an anomaly.

Will Japan's role in Asia change in the next decade? At least three different roles seem plausible. Japan might once again become an active participant in Asian *Realpolitik*. Or, like the once-great second-rank powers of western Europe, it may remain politically introverted and militarily dependent. Or it may attain a larger role in Asia primarily by nonmilitary means.

The three essays in this booklet explore these models of Japan's future and their implications for American foreign policy. A complete construction of possible futures would describe systematically a great number of variables pertaining to internal and external developments in Japan, the United States, China, the Soviet Union, and Southeast Asian countries and postulate the many interactions of these variables to each other. But these essays are not exercises in prediction or model building. With various admixtures of evidence, intuition, and speculation, the authors emphasize particular factors and trends so as to highlight basic patterns of developments.

ROBERT E. OSGOOD
Director
Washington Center of Foreign
Policy Research

CONTENTS

JAPAN AND THE UNITED STATES IN ASIA

Studies in International Affairs Number 8

I. JAPAN AND THE UNITED STATES IN ASIA

by Robert E. Osgood

In the next decade America's position in Asia is bound to be closely linked to Japan, whose position is difficult to foresee. Its historic role, its great potential as a military power, and the vitality of its people point toward Japan's re-emergence as a major, active participant in the international politics of Asia. Yet Japan's postwar antimilitarism and its aversion to power politics on the grand scale are immense obstacles to such a role. In this circumstance one seeks clues to Japan's future in trends of Japanese opinion as much as in historical precedents or in the changing nature of the international environment.

An important, although still small, segment of Japanese opinion is represented by a group of academicians and journalists who approach problems of international politics in a new vein of realism about issues of power and national interests.[1] The

[1] It would be invidious to mention names, but anyone familiar with the current ferment in Japanese thinking and writing about foreign and military questions will know the group to which I refer. Lacking insight into the deep undercurrents of Japanese thinking that others detect, I have taken their views pretty much at face value. My generalizations should be regarded as composite impressions, subject to all the qualifications that would pertain to a similar group in the United States. I initially derived these impressions from eleven days of intensive discussions with leading Japanese journalists and academicians in December 1966. Since then, I have followed their views in the Japanese press (particularly the *Chuo-Koron*) and in personal discussions.

very existence of this group (which, for convenience, I shall call the analysts) is a significant development of the last three or four years—perhaps more significant than the specific views its members have been expounding. Anyone inquiring into Japan's future role in Asia must examine carefully the views of Japan's most articulate analysts of power politics, while recognizing that their views may be more significant as a harbinger of Japan's return to *Realpolitik* than as a forecast of specific policies.

The analysts are moderate, pragmatic, relatively objective publicists who have taken a leading role in discussions of political and military issues that were only recently taboo in Japan. They are proud of their realism and eager to advance it against the dead weight of prevailing leftist-neutralist-pacifist thought. Increasingly, they gain a hearing in Japan's widely circulating press. If Japan is going to embark on a more active but reasoned and realistic role in international politics—as opposed to a policy based on rightist or leftist extremism dictated by sentiment and ideology—this group will provide the intellectual foundation for such a policy. But whatever the group's future influence may be, its views raise questions of great pertinence to the roles of Japan and the United States in Asia.

Feeling that Japan's long period of introversion since World War II is coming to an end, the analysts are in the vanguard of Japan's search for an active foreign policy. But they have not yet made up their minds about the particulars of Japan's future position in Asia, and they are keenly conscious of the domestic obstacles that may prevent their country from playing a large role.

Japan's new interest in international politics arises from widespread recognition that the center of international tensions is rapidly shifting to Asia and that a nation of Japan's great prosperity and latent power cannot escape the consequences of this development by trying to insulate itself from the mainstream of Asian politics. The principal events arousing this new interest are the war in Vietnam, China's development of nuclear weapons, and the Red Guard movement in China. These events have touched off a trend of thought which will eventually lead to a full-scale reassessment of Japanese foreign policy, but which now raises anxious questions (chiefly about *American* foreign policy) among thoughtful Japanese. These questions reflect a general uneasiness about U.S. application of containment policies in Asia.

The analysts' uneasiness is ambivalent. On the one hand, they recognize—explicitly or implicitly—that American military power in a general way is essential to security and order in the whole Asian-Pacific area, and they sense that Japan has a large stake—most tangibly in economic terms—in such security and order. Feeling vaguely menaced by China's recent domestic fanaticism and its growing nuclear strength, they want the United States to maintain an effective check against whatever dangers these developments may hold. Some express concern that the United States might, in a wave of neoisolationism and disaffection with the Vietnam war, become "undercommitted" in Asia in the future. All are convinced that the security treaty with the United States reflects common, not just American, interests and that even the increasingly agitated issue of the American administration of Okinawa must be resolved with due attention to the important if diminishing security value of that base.

On the other hand, they are afraid that the United States may over-react militarily to China's militant posture. They are afraid that a misguided effort to apply methods of containment that worked in Europe may lead the United States to slight the non-military elements of security and stability in Asia and to neglect positive ways of encouraging the moderation of Chinese foreign policy. (Like a number of China specialists in this country, they stress China's military weakness and the "defensive" nature of its foreign policy.) They are apprehensive that the United States may still be moved by what they believe to have been the naive anticommunist crusade of the Dulles period. They sense that U.S. involvement in Vietnam may be the prelude to an extension of containment in Asia, and they fear that such an extension would be ineffective and dangerous. Although they want an American military "presence" in the Asian-Pacific area, they want it to be as unobtrusive as possible.

The analysts' views on the war in Vietnam are similar to those held by well-informed, anxious, reluctant, and pessimistic American observers of the U.S. effort. Many explicitly appreciate the future value of the U.S. demonstration of will and ability to use force against communist revolutionary intervention in Asia, even if they think the Vietnam effort will fail.

Although the analysts are principally concerned with the effects of specific events in Vietnam and China on *American* policy, their concern reflects a growing interest in the development of a Japanese policy. This interest arises from the desire of an energetic, modern-minded intelligentsia to have its country achieve a respectable independent national role after too long a period of withdrawal from the world. In their effort to promote this role, however, they feel frustrated by the constraints upon an active Japanese foreign policy. Three constraints are particularly frustrating: (1) the pacifistic inhibitions and revulsion from power politics created by World War II; (2) the constitutional prohibitions against a military role beyond that of "self-defense," which is popularly defined in narrow, technologically anachronistic terms; (3) the internal political division between the conservative governing party and the large leftist group, which precludes a domestic consensus.

Consequently, although the analysts have recently overcome postwar taboos against writing about power politics in Asia, they are still inhibited from thinking much about such matters beyond limits felt to be compatible with domestic constraints and the development of a consensus. Although advocating a larger political role for Japan in Asia, they have left the specific nature of that role largely unexplored and have concentrated their attention on measures that fall far short of Japan's participation in an Asian military balance of power. Economic assistance and cooperation in Southeast Asia, the improvement of communications with China, participation in an international peacekeeping force, or the establishment of a league of major non-nuclear states with nuclear potential are the kinds of policies they principally envisage.

Of course, their failure to speculate about specific Japanese foreign policies in terms of the power politics of a great state reflects the lack of an im-

5

mediate incentive to examine hypothetical problems. More particularly, it reflects their reluctance to consider a Japanese military role beyond one of narrowly conceived self-defense. Although a large political role is traditionally difficult to divorce from military considerations, those who strongly advocate a larger political role for Japan are apt to insist on rejecting its military implications, as if to refute the implications that critics might draw from their advocacy. Consequently, their political prescriptions neglect the ingredient of power that has been historically essential to the foreign policy of states that would play a major role in international politics.

Yet the analysts are familiar with the considerations of military strategy and psychology that the United States must take into account in coping with China's nuclear force. Where these kinds of considerations can be reconciled with Japan's self-defense, they feel free to explore the rudiments of a Japanese military policy. Thus they see no overwhelming political obstacle to Japan's acquisition of an ABM system if Japan's security against Chinese nuclear blackmail should require it and if economic and technical considerations permit it. Few if any of the analysts see value in ABMs now, but some exhibit considerable interest in the whole ABM issue, as though eager to explore an area of advanced military technology that does not carry the stigma of advanced offensive weapons.

The analysts acknowledge Japan's considerable capacity to produce nuclear weapons, but few seem willing to advocate the exploitation of this capacity as a lever in foreign policy. None openly argues that it is desirable or politically feasible for Japan to produce nuclear weapons. Some believe that Japan's production of nuclear weapons would diminish security by making Japan more susceptible to attack and by frightening and antagonizing other Asian states. However, some also say that the acquisition of nuclear weapons is a question that deserves continual analysis in the light of international and technical developments. Most believe that India's deployment of a nuclear force would compel reconsideration of Japan's non-nuclear status.

The analysts' reluctance to contemplate a Japanese military policy related to external interests is in accord with their general depreciation of the role of military power in the politics of Asia. Although they think of themselves as realists and often cite their debt to Morgenthau's *Politics Among Nations,* they go further than American liberals of the same persuasion in complaining about the "militarization" of containment and in avowing the decisive importance of nonmilitary factors in international politics. Whereas many American liberals think of military containment and measures to moderate Chinese behavior as complementary policies and draw analogies to U.S.-Soviet relations, the Japanese analysts are inclined to view these policies as alternatives. This emphasis on nonmilitary factors enables them to envisage a more important role for Japan in an area in which Japan displays great economic strength and general vitality.

One would gather from the prevalance of this outlook that if Japan is to assume a larger military role, it will probably be the outgrowth of a gradual expansion of political and economic interests in Asia rather than the result of a sudden desire to improve Japan's military position. But now they explicitly foresee only a larger nonmilitary role for Japan.

In geopolitical terms some would envision Japan's expanding political role as a natural outgrowth of a position in Asia that is analogous to the classic British position in Europe. Evidently, this view reflects their sense that Japan is a mighty insular trading state that looks across the oceans for its sustenance—and, perhaps (if the analogy extends to the twentieth century), for its basic political attachments—rather than toward involvements on the Asian mainland. How Japan should go about preserving a balance of power in Asia without independent military power, and what particular strategies and quid pro quos should govern Japan's relations with China and Russia, are questions that remain unanswered—indeed scarcely asked.

The analysts' formulation of Japan's policy toward China goes little beyond the objectives of increasing Sino-Japanese communications, obtaining a seat for China in the U.N., and encouraging internal forces of moderation by largely unspecified means. Their policy toward Russia recognizes the advantages for Japan inherent in the Sino-Soviet split and the U.S.-Soviet détente. They anticipate the possibility that Russia may seek Japan's cooperation against China but are determined that Russia, which they seem to distrust more than China, should pay a substantial price for this cooperation. They do not speculate about the specific terms of cooperation and are quite skeptical about the possibility of an eventual Russo-Japanese alliance.

India receives negligible attention in their political outlook, since it has lost much of the power and status it had when Nehru championed nonalignment. They recognize that Nehru's formula is obsolete, but they have not yet considered the full implications of India's gradual turn toward *Realpolitik*, heralded by pragmatic Indian realists like themselves. Indonesia attracts more attention than India, but they do not yet think of it as a participant in a balance of power in which Japan has a vital interest.

These outward-looking men see Japan becoming more active in the economic and political affairs of Southeast Asia, but their notions of Japanese policy are inchoate. Some envision a special nonmilitary role for Japan in organizing forms of political cooperation among the nonaligned states near China while the United States continues to hold the outer ring with its military power. Remnants of the missionary aspect of Japan's Greater Co-Prosperity Sphere linger in the notion of a special Japanese responsibility for the development of Southeast Asia, but a number of analysts who have studied and visited this area are keenly aware of its heterogeneity and backwardness. Although these specialists may sense a vague racial kinship with other Asians, they feel no basic political or cultural affinity with the states or peoples of the area. On the other hand, they do identify with the most advanced states of the world.

Their view of Japanese-American relations is more concrete. Here they see a fundamental identity of security interests as the basis of an enduring alliance. They are uneasy about the future U.S. course in Asia and are opposed to serving as an Asian sponsor for American policy. Yet they do not speculate much about the consequences for Japanese-American relations of the growth of China's nuclear force, coupled with the resurgence of Japanese national individuality. They do not rankle under America's diplomatic and military dominance (aside from the Okinawan question), if only because they have just begun to develop a Japanese foreign policy and do not contemplate a Japanese military policy. When invited to consider Japan's future relationship with the United States in comparison to the relationships between the United States and its European allies, they do not think that theirs will follow the pattern of either France or West Germany. Some profess the view, which has been stated by American officials, that Japanese-American relations will be more nearly like Anglo-American relations—only without the intangible affinities.

At this early stage in Japan's search for a foreign policy, predictions about the nature of its role in Asia are premature, but it is interesting to speculate about probablities. It is at least not improbable that Japan's foreign policy will take a direction congenial to the incipient aspirations and the basic outlook of the analysts, but one that will go beyond their present formulations.

Conceivably, a leftist Japanese government would pursue a Nehru-like course of nonalignment and seek an entente with China, or with both China and Russia if the Sino-Soviet split should heal. More likely, Japan under any kind of government may remain content simply to hide under America's protection and enjoy prosperity without risking the domestic strife and foreign burdens that might accompany pursuit of an active role in Asia. Yet a number of factors militate against either course: Japan's basic energy and dynamism as an outward-looking nation; its geopolitical interest in an Asian balance of power and access to the sea lanes around the continent; China's hegemonial ambitions; China's prospective effort to intimidate and neutralize Japan or, possibly, to stimulate Japanese nationalism as a means of undermining the American alliance; Japan's immense wealth and latent power compared to any other potential Asian noncommunist counterpoise to China; the declining appeal of nonalignment accompanying the death or demise of its champions; the increasing attention commanded by intraregional problems of security and competition; the moderation of U.S.-Soviet competition; and the likely desire of other states, including the United States and the Soviet Union, to gain Japanese cooperation and recruit Japan on their side of a balance of power. Even a leftist government would probably have to come to terms with these factors.

The revival of Japanese confidence and pride, in combination with the above-mentioned considerations, could lead Japan to discover its future role as a major participant in a multipolar Asian balance of power, within which it would hope to restrain both China and Russia, foster the development of regional economic and political cooperation, and maintain alignments with at least India and Australia while preserving the Japanese-American alliance on the basis of a revised division of responsibilities. This possibility raises interesting questions about America's position in Asia in the coming decades.

Japan's role in an Asian balance of power would have to be preceded by the expansion of its economic relations, a trend which has already begun. Further Japanese programs and initiatives in economic assistance and regional economic cooperation (such as those already undertaken in matching the U.S. contribution to the Asian Development Bank and in calling a Tokyo conference of Southeast Asian economic ministers) seem likely to enhance Japan's status as the most advanced Asian power, legitimize her role as an active participant in Asian affairs, and promote communication on all levels with neighboring governments and peoples. The extension of economic relations should lead to a more extensive communication on general political matters between Japan and states with mutual economic interests, beginning, perhaps, with multilateral meetings like the Asian and Pacific Conference of 1966 in Seoul. Finally, the establishment of Japan as the major noncommunist Asian power might lead to increasing bilateral diplomatic relations on matters closer to *Grosspolitik*, not only with the noncommunist Asian and Pacific states but also with Russia and (depending on the nature of the regime) with China.

Japan might try to achieve a rapprochement with China or even promote a détente between China and the United States, but without a dramatic shift of Chinese policy such efforts seem doomed to fail. In any event, China probably will view Japan as a rival and as an obstacle to its territorial, hegemonial, and ideological objectives; and it will exert continual pressure to break Japan away from its American tie. Regardless of its insular safety from an invasion of the home islands, Japan can scarcely avoid regarding China as a security threat, at least in the waters between Korea and Taiwan, because Japan is bound to be the main target of any Chinese nuclear blackmail.

The Soviet Union will probably seek Japan's economic assistance and political cooperation in order to strengthen its own position against China and to gain access, through Japan, to Asian politics. In return, Japan should be able to exact Soviet good behavior and perhaps more tangible concessions with respect to Sakhalin and other islands. It might also be able to use a closer relationship with Russia to enhance its independence in dealings with the United States.

Japan will probably develop a special political alignment with India, Australia, and Indonesia (if this chaotic country should enjoy a reasonably moderate and responsible government), based on mutual interests in the restraint of Chinese influence and the promotion of regional cooperation and stability. The geographical remoteness and special interests of these states will render their alignments of only limited military import, but Japanese materiel and technical military assistance might provide tangible support to alignments.

Given a modicum of stability and security in Southeast Asia, Japan would probably become the major participant in the economic development of the area. By this means it would gain international status and respectability while contributing to the security of the area against communist penetration and subversion. At the same time, Japan's growing economic role in the region would enlarge its political role and stake in Southeast Asia.

All these political developments would be consistent with Japan's maintenance of its alliance with the United States. The alliance, of course, would be contingent upon a degree of convergence between Japan's policies and American interests; and the United States, as the military partner and superpower, would control the outer limits of Japan's political arena. But this very circumstance might reassure Asian states of Japan's good behavior, somewhat as the American alliance in Europe has served that function with respect to West Germany. If so, the alliance would facilitate Japan's expanding political role.

Yet within the U.S.-Japanese alliance Japan's developing political role would surely lead to an increasing differentiation between Japanese and American foreign policies in Asia. It seems unlikely that the closer military and political entanglement of the United States and Germany during the rise of Soviet nuclear power will be reproduced in American-Japanese relations as China's nuclear force grows. Japan operates under no comparable imperative of security or reunification. It is more likely that Japan will try to enhance its security and influence by independent diplomatic and military means than by tighter military integration with the United States. As technological developments permit and political expediency requires the United States to project its military power to the mainland from Pacific bases and positions that are less politically sensitive, there will undoubtedly be devolution of responsibility for the defense of the Japanese islands from the United States to Japan.

If Japan were to assume a more active economic and political role in Asia, the question of whether it should protect and advance its expanded interests with military power would then come to the forefront. The Japanese may then regard their security and influence as sufficiently assured without their own military backing. Undertaking a military role larger than one of self-defense may well seem too divisive internally and too provocative externally to be worth the hypothetical advantages. Yet it would certainly be one of the great anomalies of history if a state with the potential power, the extensive foreign interests, the long-run security problem, and the national vitality of Japan should indefinitely entrust the military protection of its interests to another state or to the vicissitudes of a military balance controlled by others. It would not be surprising, therefore, if the expansion of Japan's political dealings and interests in Asia were to lead to an expansion of Japan's conception of its security interests and military policies. The very process of developing an active foreign policy might create a domestic consensus about, and foreign acceptance of, Japan's military participation in some fashion in an Asian balance of power. This depends very much on the skill and tact of Japanese diplomacy and on whether the United States, the Soviet Union, and other states find Japan's growing influence useful to them.

If Japan were to develop an independent military policy to support its expanded political interests, that policy would probably gain its initial impetus from the formulation of special security interests with respect to Korea and Taiwan. It might then develop a broader commitment to cooperate with regional alignments like the Association of Southeast Asian Nations (ASEAN). Eventually, Japan's increased diplomatic activities might convince the government that its political weight in Asia should be enhanced by a capacity to project military power beyond the passive defense of its borders.

Would the expansion of Japan's military role include the acquisition of nuclear weapons? The answer to this question depends on a great many factors: technical and economic considerations, domestic opinion and politics, the political use that China tries to make of its nuclear weapons, America's technical and strategic response to China's nuclear force, the extent of American support for major Japanese policies, the apparent political efficacy or inefficacy of France's nuclear force, India's or Australia's production or nonproduction of nuclear weapons, the utility and political acceptability of Japan's deployment of ABM's, and the attitude of the United States, the Soviet Union, and China toward a prospective Japanese nuclear force.

Would a lafger Japanese military role in Asia lead to a new system of military alliances? Probably the condition and consequence of such a role would be the extension of Japanese military commitments and ties in some form, but the political heterogeneity of the area precludes the development of a full-blown system of military alliances as in nineteenth-century Europe. Nonetheless, one can realistically envision Japan forming limited guarantee pacts and mutual assistance agreements with India and Indonesia and entering military assistance agreements, making unilateral declarations of military intent, and contracting various kinds of military understandings with some lesser Asian powers.

The prospect, however remote, of Japan's emergence as an active participant in an Asian balance of power raises the question of what U.S. long-run policy toward this prospect should be. Until now U.S. policy in the Asian-Pacific area has been dominated by the attempt to contain China. Few responsible critics of containment argue that American interests do not require checking the expansion of China and allied communist parties. The controversies about containment in Asia, as in Europe, have revolved around the urgency, desirability, and feasibility of the *means* of containment, especially when the question of American military intervention arises. Although containment will remain a compelling objective in Asia, it is likely to be less and less adequate as the total description of a fruitful American policy. The configurations of national interest and power in Asia are too complicated, inchoate, and loosely organized to fit the pattern of a revisionist state or coalition organized against a group of status quo powers. Even in terms of the remnants of the cold war, China's independent position creates a kind of tripolarity. Moreover, as in Europe, the more successful or less urgent containment may become, the more complicated the patterns of international politics and the more decisive international relationships other than containment are likely to become. And in Asia, too, there looms the long-run problem of promoting not only an equilibrium of power within which change can take place without threatening international order but also, if feasible, an equilibrium that does not depend on the direct presence of preponderant American force.

It would be unfortunate if preoccupation with containing China led to the neglect of other policy objectives and problems. Yet it would be disastrous if an emotional preference for the more "positive," nonmilitary aspects of international politics led to neglect of the imperatives of containment. Therefore it would be a serious mistake to draw from the obvious fact that political and military conditions in Asia are different from those in Europe, the common conclusion—popular in the United States as well as in Japan—that containment is inapplicable to Asia.

We must expect that China, united under a communist regime, will continue to follow expansionist policies, even if it eschews direct military aggression. It has avowed national territorial objectives that it aspires to acquire by force and intimidation if possible, it has more general ambitions of hegemonic influence in Asia, and it has ideological-nationalist goals that look toward the establishment of pro-Chinese communist parties and states through revolutionary violence.

Military power is an indispensable and primary instrument of Chinese policy, but China is now very weak militarily. It has, furthermore, always been cautious to avoid the direct use of its military power except for the defense of its territory. American military power has made this weakness evident, has reinforced this caution, and has encouraged states that might otherwise be vulnerable to China's armed forces or allied revolutionary organizations to withstand intimidation and subversion. Thus American military power has evidently deterred China from carrying out its designs against Taiwan and has helped to limit China's assistance to the Viet Minh in the Vietnam war. It has enabled Burma and Cambodia, by the testimony of their leaders, to retain their independence as nonaligned states, it has been a major factor in the uneasy "neutralization" of Laos, and it may have been a background factor in the willingness of Indonesians to suppress an attempted communist takeover.

Of course, the American military presence in the Asian-Pacific area makes China's leaders feel that the United States is encircling China. In China's somewhat paranoid perspective, containment may appear to be preparation for an eventual military attack. These reactions to American policy undoubtedly reinforce China's view that its cautious pursuit of what it regards as legitimate, predestined, external goals is essentially defensive. Soviet leaders seem to have been motivated by something of this same defensive-offensive psychology. This is not the first time that states convinced of the necessity and righteousness of their hegemony have viewed opposition to their mission as an offensive threat to their vital interests. But it does not follow that, in the absence of containment, China would abstain from intervening in the surrounding areas or be less militant. Nor does it follow that containment need provoke China into rash actions. The objective evidence of both Chinese and Soviet responses to military counterpoises indicates that, in the long run, the best inducement to their moderation is their discovery that the prospect of forceful opposition makes offensive adventures ineffective, costly, and risky. There is reason to think that Chinese, like Soviet, leaders will eventually moderate their ambitions and strategies if they are continually confronted with failure. And the present Chinese regime's extravagant vision of "people's revolutions" sweeping over underdeveloped areas seems productive of failure wherever China or its most ambitious proxies are unable to support revolutions with force. In any case, the United States cannot afford to make the primary object of its policy the alleviation of fears and frustrations of states that seek to change the status quo through force.

Regardless of the outcome of the Vietnam war, containment seems to be a necessary ingredient of American policy in the Asian-Pacific area unless China should become so weak from civil strife as to become a negligible power. But containment is clearly not enough. Even now the United States badly needs a policy for international order in Asia—a policy that transcends the containment of China and yet is relevant to the concrete problems of security and stability. It needs a policy with which Asian states that are beginning to grapple with the realities of international politics can identify their interests.

Yet in the aftermath of the Vietnam war, despite the inevitable reluctance of Americans to become involved in another such intervention, there may be a tendency for the United States to extend its commitments in Asia as part of a more comprehensive application of containment intended to prevent a recurrence of such a war. That is what happened after the Korean War and the war in Indochina. The sweeping rhetoric of President Johnson's efforts to present the Vietnam war in a larger context and to rally Asian support have already led—probably misled—American and foreign observers to conclude that the United States looks toward the creation of a grand Asian coalition on the European pattern, with an Asian version of the Marshall Plan thrown in to sweeten the military pill.

Quite apart from the military and economic burdens of such an expansion of containment, one must view with consternation the political difficulties and disadvantages of the U.S. attempt to undertake in Asia anything resembling what was achieved in Europe. Yet perhaps the alternative consistent with American interests, *if* China is strong enough to require a counterpoise, is the fostering of a multipolar balance of power in which the United States could find a more specialized, less predominant, more politically appropriate, and less direct involvement than is likely to develop if China and the Soviet Union are the only other major centers of power in Asia. Here, of course, is where Japan enters the scene, because Japan's active participation in Asian politics is clearly indispensable to the emergence of an advantageous multipolar balance.

Furthermore, the prospect of a multipolar balance bears directly upon the position of China. It is now almost universal doctrine that China should be contained but not isolated. The latter half of this apothegm states either a politically meaningless or dubious proposition if it presupposes some special utility in greater official and unofficial contacts with China apart from the nature of Chinese foreign policy, or if it assumes that such contacts will by themselves and regardless of their substance moderate Chinese policy. The idea—popular in Japan as well as in the United States—that China's U.N. membership will either break down her isolation or moderate her foreign policy seems especially far-fetched considering the great variety of policies and degrees of international isolation or involvement among both members and nonmembers of that organization. On the other hand, if China's emergence from a largely self-imposed isolation should be the product of a more active and normal diplomatic relationship with other states, that relationship might well expose it to the kind of influence and give its leaders the kinds of incentives that would encourage a more realistic and moderate policy. This kind of diplomatic relationship is far more likely to develop within a multipolar balance of power in which China must seek an advantage by maneuvering among several centers of power than in a tripolar balance in which China's interests are preoccupied with the opposition to one great capitalist enemy in collusion with an heretical communist colossus.

But this is not the place to speculate about the details of a multipolar balance, nor to weigh its hypothetical advantages against all its probable disadvantages. My purpose here is simply to suggest how the future roles of the United States and Japan in Asia depend upon the future structure of power.

At present, U.S. policy toward Japan's future role in Asia seems as rudimentary and ambivalent as the analysts' view of that role. In part, this situation exists because although the American government appreciates that the containment formulas suitable to Europe are not entirely appropriate in Asia, it has not developed a coherent vision of a broader strategy of security compatible with the objectives of containment.

On the one hand, American representatives are urging Japan to break out of its unrealistic thralldom to isolation and pacifism. Their urging springs from several sources: In their view Japan, a thriving nation with great power potential, is receiving all the benefits of its alliance with the United States without carrying a proper share of burdens and responsibilities for either its own defense or the security and stability of Asia. They also feel that if Japan were to assume a greater role in Asian affairs, it would develop greater realism about the problems of power that concern the United States and would therefore be easier to deal with. As in the American view toward Europe, there is a feeling that psychologically and politically it is better to have a strong and independent "partner" than a frustrated and somewhat irresponsible dependent (given the assumed basic identity of interests). In western Europe the application of this view was largely confined to the promotion of a "united Europe," which was seen as a barrier to revival of the separate European nationalisms that had involved the United States in two world wars. But in Asia Japan stands alone as a potentially powerful ally. Related to the alleged advantages of more nearly equal partnership is the view that Japan's adoption of a realistic, active foreign policy may provide the best antidote to the neutralist-leftist view of policy, on the one hand, and to the mobilization of resurgent nationalism against the United States, on the other.

Perhaps more important than these considerations is the U.S. reluctance to carry the whole burden of power politics in Asia. Americans have never welcomed an extension of commitments, despite the fact that they have accepted a remarkable sequence of unanticipated extensions because there seemed to be no alternative compatible with containment. Their consciousness of Asia's great heterogeneity and backwardness; their lack of cultural, political, and racial affinity with Asian peoples; and ironic remnants of the historic principle of keeping American boys out of Asia make further entanglement in this area particularly unwelcome. Moreover, there is less prospect of the kind of regional initiative and cooperation in Asia that made the extension of American commitments to Europe politically acceptable and even attractive. Then, too, looking toward the 1970s when China may be a more impressive conventional military power with nuclear weapons capable of reaching American cities, some Americans are concerned about the problems of maintaining single-handedly the efficacy of deterrence against China and of preserving the confidence of other states in the American deterrent. The prospect of guaranteeing the security of India and of reinforcing American guarantees to Japan in compensation for their nuclear abstention adds to this concern. Analogous problems in Europe have been difficult enough, but at least there the United States has been able to reinforce the credibility of its commitment with its standing forces and its leadership of an institutionalized military alliance.

Finally, American reluctance to be the preponderant guarantor of Asian security stems from the agony and frustration of the Vietnam war and the adverse domestic reaction to it. Whatever the results of this war, Americans will want their government to be more cautious about underwriting other Asian countries with military support. Yet having endured the Vietnam war under the banner of the Truman Doctrine and having supported South Vietnam as a crucial domino in Asia, the United States cannot very well leave all the dominoes to themselves or decline to support others that appeal for American assistance. In any case, one of the legacies of the Vietnam war seems likely to be the continuation for some time of a sizable American presence in the area to strengthen and guarantee the "free peoples" who wish to resist "attempted subjugation by armed minorities or by outside pressures." It is not clear exactly how Japan or any other advanced state can contribute to the security of Southeast Asia against indirect aggression, except through economic assistance, some kinds of military aid, and closer political contact. No one yet anticipates a Japanese military role for this purpose. Nevertheless, there will be a growing tendency for the United States to seek a greater Japanese engagement in the area as a major contribution to building a regional framework of security in which the United States can undertake more limited responsibilities.

On the other hand, in the light of World War II, Americans view the emergence of Japan as an in dependent active force in international politics with the same uneasiness inspired by the prospect of West Germany's resurgence. A militant leftist government in Japan would be especially disturbing. At present, fears of Japanese militarism, expansionism, or leftist-nationalism are quite muted. But the mere prospect of Japan as an active full-scale great power with an unresolved political schism is disturbing.

There is another reason why Americans are inclined to worry about the addition of any major center of power to the international system, almost regardless of its internal complexion or foreign orientation: Additional centers of independent military decisions threaten to reduce the U.S. capacity to choose the conditions under which it will incur the risks of war and to increase the chance of war by political miscalculation. The still largely bipolar world (in a military sense), after many anxious moments, has come to look like a relatively safe and manageable one. A multipolar world international system, even if confined to Asia, would complicate problems of security and stable deterrence. It would be bound to make international life look more dangerous.

Americans have no experience with or historical memories of the United States as a world power participating in a multipolar system comparable to the European systems of the eighteenth or nineteenth centuries. Some Americans fear the prospect, but others welcome it as a means of reducing American commitments and mitigating some political burdens. Yet American support for multipolarity may be based on premises that would occasion rapid disillusionment if real multipolarity were to develop. In light of the U.S. role in the cold war as the leader of an anticommunist coalition, Americans are inclined to view multipolarity merely as a more loosely organized coalition in which other states would make a larger independent contribution to collective security. In line with their ideal image of a "pluralistic" world, they are inclined to overestimate the harmony of interests among the poles of power.

It remains to be seen whether the United States is prepared to support the resurgence of a Japan pursuing policies that diverge from its own with the same enthusiasm that some Americans display now, when Japan has scarcely developed a foreign policy. Would a strong and independent Japan be a partner like Britain? Japan under a strong nationalist regime, which may be the essential condition for achieving a domestic consensus to support an active foreign policy, might look more like France under de Gaulle—but with considerably more influence in the relatively weak and unstructured Asian field of power than France can exert in Europe. Among Americans who anxiously scan the Asian horizon this disquieting thought lingers in uneasy juxtaposition with predominantly optimistic views about an American-Japanese partnership.

Of course, the ambivalence in the American attitude toward Japan's hypothetical emergence as an active major power may be inconsequential in practice. China may remain too weak to pose any problem in constructing a balance of power, and Japan may remain inhibited from playing the full role of a great power in Asia. The decisive forms of power may not depend on high-level military cooperation among Asian states—as long as the United States keeps the Seventh Fleet and some bases in the Asian-Pacific area—but rather on the kind of economic and political relations that Japan is now beginning to promote.

On the other hand, tendencies in other directions could confront the United States with rather sharp and uncomfortable policy dilemmas. Suppose, for example, that Japan's acquisition of nuclear weapons were to become a serious prospect. Americans might welcome the addition of an Asian counterpoise to China's nuclear force, provided that Japan's foreign policies were congenial with American policies. But if Japan regarded the reduction of American influence in Asia and the pursuit of an independent policy as primary objectives of an independent nuclear force, few Americans could be expected to favor this. At present the issue has scarcely arisen. The nuclear taboo is still much too strong. Consequently, American representatives (including most of those who want Japan to play a major role in Asian politics) are inclined to view the prospect of a Japanese nuclear force in the context of general opposition to nuclear proliferation. In this context, those who do not view an hypothetical Japanese nuclear force as dangerous or politically disturbing in itself are nevertheless opposed to it and eager to have Japan take the lead in nonproliferation; they fear that Japan's production of nuclear weapons would lead other states to build nuclear forces, including West Germany. But let us suppose that Japan were a major participant in Asian politics and that the constructive nationalist forces encouraged by the United States were, for any number of conceivable reasons, approaching a choice between either a Japanese nuclear force or additional American guarantees, some kind of nuclear sharing and the like. Would the U.S. opposition to nuclear proliferation (presumably, by then, embodied in a treaty) take precedence over all other considerations of security and diplomacy? Should it?

The dilemma posed by this hypothetical and, at present, seemingly improbable development suggests that the one question now largely suppressed in discussions of Japan's role in Asia could someday become the key question: What is to be the nature of Japan's military role? American ambivalence toward Japan's emergence from isolation need not entail contradictions in policy *if* Japan can make a major contribution to a stable balance of power in Asia without a military force to back it up beyond the defense of Japan itself. This is evidently the hope of most American observers, as well as of the Japanese analysts. They may be right, but there is little evidence in the history of balances of power to substantiate their hope.

II. LIVING WITH THE REAL JAPAN
by George R. Packard III

In the first century of our relations with Japan, both countries swung from extremes of high hope to despair, and back again to hope. Now, with greater opportunities to know each other and with a dialogue reopened between our intellectuals, there should be wiser calculations on both sides of the Pacific. Instead, we are again moving in different directions and, at least for the moment, there is the danger that high expectations will again founder on misunderstandings.

It is not surprising that we are badly informed about Japan. Our press coverage of the major power in Asia and the third greatest industrial power in the world is absurdly inadequate. Only one of the regular American correspondents in Tokyo can speak and read Japanese usefully. American editors seem determined to limit all stories on Japan to the exotic, inscrutable, or threatening. Scholarly works, with few exceptions, are becoming increasingly specialized. Despite new attention to East Asia in college and high school courses, it is still hard for the layman to find out what he needs to know about our most important and difficult Asian ally.

The Japanese, it should be added, have done little better. Members of their press corps in Washington speak English badly as a rule, and reach few important sources. Their editors favor critics of the administration without giving equal space to majority views. Japanese visitors tend to be subjective and emotional when they record their impressions of the United States, and scholars are often specialized like our own or committed to a viewpoint before they arrive. Because of the occupation and our continuing physical presence in Japan, it is easy for Japanese to feel they know us when often they are dealing in false images.

It may be that we can each survive our misapprehensions, letting the diplomats try to untangle the knots, but it would seem better to try to get the picture in focus now than to face a new round of frustrations later on.

The argument of this essay is that, while the United States should do what it can to influence Japan to emerge from its shell and help build a more stable and prosperous Asia, the very effort to use our influence may be fruitless at best and could produce opposite results at worst.

Americans who contend that Japan has now become a great power, or will soon become one, and in the next breath urge Japan to build up its arms, intervene politically in Southeast Asia, contribute to a U.N. peacekeeping force, or otherwise adapt itself to U.S. policy objectives are caught in a contradiction. The occupation is over. Our habit of telling the Japanese where their interests lie must be broken. Japan, as a great power and free society, will follow its own inner urgings, and it is in the U.S. national interest to relax and let the Japanese work out their own destiny, free of the fear that they are simply following along as American puppets acting out an American strategy in Asia.

There is a new myth in Washington that Japan is beginning to wake up to the responsibilities of adulthood after fifteen years of passive dependence on American power. According to this myth, an economically resurgent, nationalistic Japan will and should play a larger political, economic, and perhaps military role in Asia, that such a role will inevitably fit in with our strategy of containing communism, and that it is mainly the political left in Japan that has been standing in the way of a more useful alliance.

As a consequence of these assumptions, there is a warm feeling in Washington each time Japan raises its defense outlay, buys more sophisticated (American) military equipment, sponsors a conference of Asian nations, or shows any other hint of wanting to become involved again in Asian politics. There is happiness when an influential journal publishes "realistic" Japanese thinking about the need for more forceful diplomacy backed by military power. We have been patient long enough, it is said, with idealistic pacifism, and it is time the Japanese were jolted from their dream world and apprised of the nasty facts of political life.

It is true, of course, that Japan has recently shown a greater willingness to take on the burden of its own sea and air defense, and that the naive pacifism of the postwar period is disappearing. But there is an enormous difference between these halting steps and full involvement in the containment of communism in Asia, and it is this distinction which our policy-makers have failed to perceive.

Ever since the outbreak of the Korean War in 1950, and particularly since 1953 when Vice-President Nixon openly urged the Japanese to change Article IX of their Constitution, the Japanese have been under pressure from Washington to increase their defense forces. They have responded, but at their own slow pace and in the spirit of former Prime Minister Yoshida, who wrote in his memoirs in 1961, "To me, the idea of rearmament has always seemed to be one verging on idiocy. . . . The necessary wealth is lacking, and, even more than wealth, the necessary psychological background."

Now that Japan seems to be moving toward "realism" about its own security (even Yoshida changed his position and advocated more arms before he died in 1967) there is a tendency in Washington to assume that, with its new muscles, Japan will help the United States balance the scale against mainland China. To the extent that a stronger, independent Japan is by itself a countervailing power, this assumption is correct. But to the extent that it envisions a stronger Japan complementing our own power in the Pacific, and helping the United States to defend weaker Asian nations against the threat of communist aggression or communist-inspired insurgencies, it is highly misleading.

We continue to urge Japan to rearm, not in specific, formal messages, but in the over-all thrust of our policies. Yet we have not clearly defined either for ourselves or for the Japanese precisely what it is that we want them to do. We like to hear them talk tough about the communist threat in Asia, but we also want them to sign the nuclear nonproliferation treaty. At the cost of demonstrations and considerable trouble for local authorities, we bring nuclear-powered submarines and the aircraft carrier *Enterprise* into Sasebo to provide rest and recreation for the crews, and as the Navy puts it, to get the Japanese over their "nuclear allergy." Yet, when the Japanese decide to build a nuclear-powered merchant ship of their own, Westinghouse is prohibited from giving Mitsubishi the necessary information on marine reactors. It is clear that we are not urging Japan to acquire nuclear arms, but it is not clear what we want them to do with their stronger conventional forces beyond defending themselves. "It seems," said one official in Japan's Defense Agency recently, "that the Pentagon wants us to play the infield while you play the outfield against the Chinese."

The hope in Washington for a stronger Japan to complement American power in the Pacific arises, understandably, from our frustration and sense of isolation in Vietnam, from our eagerness to share the burden, from our conviction that Asians should be more interested in their own security, and from our feeling that the Japanese have had a long free ride. But it runs headlong into the mood of Japan today.

The essential point about Japan and the United States today is that while we are deeply involved in Asia, the Japanese, despite a few tentative and cautious moves toward regional cooperation, are absorbed more than ever in their own domestic problems. Ironically, it is partly because we *are* the predominant power in Asia that Japan abstains from playing the role in Asia that its economic power could support.

Japan's introspective mood should not be surprising. Critics who charge that its foreign policy is figured on an abacus tend to forget the wrenching changes that rapid modernization has brought to Japan, and to overlook the tensions in Japanese society that still persist from the war, total defeat and occupation.

Far from designing a bolder foreign policy, the Japanese are trying to cope with problems involved in rapid urbanization, the huge gulfs between generations, civilian rule, the shallow bases of political parties, the democratic process in a hierarchical society, the role of the individual where the group prevails, the breakup of the traditional family structure and the loss of an entire value system. For the first time they are enjoying each other—even their domestic squabbles—liberated in an explosion of energy from rigid class divisions and police-state repression. Although there has been no great social upheaval, the prewar military and imperial household elites have suddenly disappeared, leaving the bureaucrats, politicians and business men to fight it out at the top.

Unlike other elite groups in Asia, Japan's leaders must respond to the popular will, and that will has made itself felt again and again: it is against war, against taking risks abroad, against rocking the boat in any way that could threaten the new prosperity, against foreign commitments that could drag Japan into a war that did not involve its immediate interests. The consumer-voter is learning to make his will felt at the polls, and the politicians are learning to respond.

Japan's "economic miracle" has left serious problems in its wake. The public sector has been neglected, and taxes, which have been going down for a decade, are scheduled to go up in the next decade. The additional revenue will go not to defense or foreign aid, but to roads, schools and hospitals. A third of Tokyo's eleven million citizens live in housing that is considered substandard, and those with decent homes still face a daily penance of smog and traffic jams. The farms are being deserted for the cities, rural poverty is widespread, small businesses are folding, larger ones are merging in the face of capital liberalization policies, the debt structure of private business is staggering, and juvenile delinquency is on the rise. This is not a nation that is about to embark on a drive to influence the rest of Asia.

Considering all these problems, the political scene has been remarkably stable. But the ruling Liberal-Democratic Party, in power for twenty years, has been more of a steward than a producer of dynamic leadership. Government policy has been set by a consensus among the new elites, and initiatives have been trimmed to the lowest common denominator. The highly competitive factions within the party tend to cut down the overly ambitious, and there is no de Gaulle or even a Thanat Khoman on the Japanese horizon. There has been broad agreement on the general guidelines for economic growth, and the factional struggles are not about what shall be done but who shall do it. It has not been the leftist intellectuals so much as the ingrained bureaucratic caution of the conservative leaders themselves that has checked new initiatives abroad.

Recent developments have further reduced opportunities for forceful leadership. The conservatives for the first time since the war, won less than 50 percent of the popular vote in the general elections of January 1967 and, despite their majority in the Diet, they will be more dependent than before on bargaining with the opposition. The "Yoshida School," of which prime ministers Ikeda and Sato have been the star alumni, has nearly run out its string, and a new generation of politicians is adding further uncertainty to the political scene. None of the leading candidates to succeed Sato is likely to carry out a significant change in foreign policy.

The leading opposition party, the Socialists, lost ground in the 1967 general elections and buried the old myth that time, youth, and urbanization would inevitably carry them to power. This and the advance of two minor parties, the Democratic Socialists and the Komeito (Soka Gakkai), with 30 and 25 seats respectively in the lower house, have opened up new possibilities for fluidity, leading perhaps to coalitions and shifting alliances—again scarcely the conditions for new undertakings abroad.

The primacy of domestic politics in Japan is evident most clearly in the fact that foreign ministers in recent years have almost all been chosen from the thick of domestic politics. They are often without experience in foreign affairs, and usually unable to speak any language but Japanese. The opposition has shown much the same concern for domestic politics: a Socialist leader travels to Moscow, Peking, or Hanoi not so much to exchange views or cement ties as to get the better of a competing domestic faction. This is not to suggest that Japan has been standing still diplomatically, but that its foreign policy reflects the popular conviction that the tasks of rebuilding and adjusting to changes at home must come first.

Japan's increased international involvement over the past three years has been more a matter of winning friends than influencing people. The major moves have been joining OECD in 1964; accepting, as a member of the Development Assistance Committee, a pledge to raise foreign aid to 1 percent of the national income; normalizing relations with the Republic of Korea in 1965; quietly opposing the Chinese communists at Algiers in 1965; calling a conference on Asian agricultural development in 1966; joining in multilateral aid to Indonesia in 1966–67; joining the Asian and Pacific Council (ASPAC); pledging $200 million to the Asian Development Bank and providing its president; and promising $100 million to the special agricultural fund in 1967. Lately Foreign Minister Miki has put forward the idea of an Asia-Pacific sphere, calling for closer consultation among the five advanced nations and the less-developed countries of the area. It would be a mistake, however, to conclude from all this that Japan is about to jump back into the power politics of Asia.

For one thing, Japan's aid to the less-developed countries was only $520 million in 1966 or 0.69 percent of national income, a slight drop from the previous year. (About half of this aid went to Asian countries.) This is a respectable showing (fifth in the free world) for a country that ranks twenty-second in the world in per capita national income. But it is not likely, even when combined with trade and technical assistance, to give Japan a major voice in Asian politics in the near future, and it is not likely to rise dramatically in the short run. Leading politicians predict that the public will strongly oppose any attempt to raise the figure substantially. Some of them even admit that the concept of Pan-Asian solidarity is more a dream of the left and right fringes than a popular guide to action.

The new relationship with the Republic of Korea brings economic benefits to both sides, but it does not necessarily fore-shadow a convergence of foreign policies and it will surely not lead, as some have speculated, to joint security arrangements. Japan joined ASPAC reluctantly, and only after the Koreans and Thais agreed not to give it a strong anticommunist coloration. As one senior Japanese diplomat put it, "We are on the extreme left in ASPAC." The Japanese role will continue to be one of blocking ASPAC from taking a strong anti-Peking line.

Nothing could illustrate Japan's wariness of political involvement with its neighbors better than a tea party that took place in Seoul on July 2, 1967. Vice-President Humphrey, Vice-President C. K. Yen of Nationalist China, and Prime Minister Sato were attending the inauguration of President Park Chung Hee, and a meeting of the four leaders was proposed. Japan agreed to attend a tea party, but only on condition that wives might also attend. The purpose of this condition, according to *Asahi Shimbun* (July 3, 1967), was to avoid the political coloration that might otherwise attach to such a gathering. Observers in Tokyo could recall no other occasion when the Japanese had been first to suggest bringing wives along.

There have, however, been three major changes of attitude in Japan that could affect foreign policy in the future. The first is the rise of national self-confidence, a continuation of the trend that began with the economic boom of the late 1950s, found expression in the security-treaty riots of 1960, was notable at the 1964 Tokyo Olympics, and continues to grow with the new generations that never knew war and defeat. The massive inferiority complex of the postwar decade has given way to a more relaxed and stable public mood. Japan no longer panics at the first rise in international tension, no longer sees its economic quarrels as affairs of national honor. With new confidence and national pride, the people have learned to live with dissension at home despite their traditional love of consensus.

The new mood seeks a greater voice for Japan at international councils, but not at the price of risky commitments or costly ventures or of going beyond Article IX, the war-renouncing clause of the Constitution. For example, while the United Nations has always been popular, any suggestion that Japan might contribute to a United Nations peacekeeping force is enough to set off a furor. The present self-defense forces have won over 80 percent public acceptance in the opinion polls, but only a small minority would like to see them strengthened. The army has never been able to recruit enough volunteers to fill its quota. The conservative leaders, far from being nostalgic about the good old days of national power, are acutely conscious of the dangers of usurpation by the military in a land that has known military supremacy for centuries. They scrutinize each new budget request from the Defense Ministry with jaundiced eyes. The new nationalism in Japan does not translate quickly or easily into a desire for more military power.

The second trend, related to the first, is an eagerness to escape from the shadow of American power, to prove to the world and to itself that Japan is not an American puppet, to disengage emotionally from the overwhelming influence that economic, military, and cultural ties have exerted in the past twenty-two years. The trend was inevitable, and even therapeutic in view of the larger-than-life role we played during the occupation and afterward. But in the last three years, uneasiness, mistrust, and, in some quarters, hostility have been added largely as a result of Vietnam.

For most Japanese, the war is seen primarily as white men shooting Asians, westerners using sophisticated weaponry against nationalists defending their homeland. Above all it is unpopular because it could lead to a wider war involving Japan, though this fear has subsided somewhat in recent months. Among Japanese leaders, other considerations have entered the picture; some of the sting is removed by our war-related spending in Japan, estimated at $600 million in 1966 and much more in 1967–68. Some leaders have been impressed by the fact that the United States appears determined to stay in Asia for the long haul. Still others are noting that, by its inability to win a quick victory, it is proving itself less than omnipotent. It is too early to say which of these calculations will be more important in the long run, and much depends on the outcome of the war.

In any event, for the first time in many years, the United States is no longer the nation best liked by the Japanese people, having been replaced by Switzerland, according to at least one poll.[1] Increasingly, our shortcomings are noted in the press while our successes are belittled or ignored. American importations which are admirable are now so familiar as to seem Japanese, while the side effects of modernization, such as juvenile delinquency, are blamed on American influence. Individualism is still suspect as profit-seeking egoism. When Stalin's daughter came

[1] Poll taken by Central Survey Institute in January 1967, published in *Shukan Jiji*, February 4, 1967.

to America, members of the establishment in Japan spoke of it in the same vein as *Pravda*: it was a CIA operation and she was unstable and greedy. A leading newsweekly ignored the story as "insignificant." When the marines entered the Demilitarized Zone in Vietnam, it was the United States that committed "dangerous escalation," not the entrenched North Vietnamese regulars.

When President Johnson was planning a visit to Korea after the Manila Conference of October 1966, consideration was given to a visit to Japan. The reaction in Tokyo was prompt: "inconceivable." The Japanese government wanted no part of a visit that would have linked it, however remotely, to American military strategy in Asia. Even today, with Prime Minister Sato having paid his second formal visit to Washington, an attempt by President Johnson to visit Tokyo would set off bloody rioting and end in cancellation. It is possible that these tensions will disappear with the end of the fighting in Vietnam, but for the moment, the U.S. government's image in Japan is at a postwar low.

The third change in attitude, also related to nationalism, is truly revolutionary: for the first time since 1949, there is widespread disillusionment with Communist China, which recently replaced the Soviet Union at the bottom of a popularity poll. Persecution of intellectuals, excesses of the Red Guards, the blatant power struggle, and Mao's unexpected fallibility have combined to reduce the former awe and respect for the Chinese revolution even among the progressive intellectuals. And the Japanese Communist Party, once putty in the hands of Peking, has declared its independence. Still, as noted below, Japanese views of the future of China are vastly different from our own.

These changes in Japanese thinking have recently permitted a group of younger intellectuals to advocate publicly a more assertive diplomacy supported by more military power and possibly even nuclear weapons—ideas that were previously taboo. The new debate, which has been cheered from the sidelines by Washington, examines Japan's potential as a Gaullist power, ponders the uncertainties of relying on the United States for long-range security, and usually accepts the premise of Japan as a "better because more independent" ally of the United States. The new realists,[2] as they are called, have exerted little influence on government leaders, who have been privately considering these arguments for years, but it may be significant that they are getting space in the journals that once belonged exclusively to the pacifist left wing. The debate has gained impetus in the past months from public discussion of the nuclear nonproliferation treaty. In a remarkable show of unity, all parties except the communists have indicated reservations about signing the treaty without commitments from the superpowers to disarm.

Yet, for all the debate, there are few important politicians in Japan today who dare openly to advocate nuclear weapons for Japan, and even the realists agree that the obstacles to joining the nuclear club are enormous. Article IX of the Constitution and the Basic Atomic Energy Law would have to be revised, at the cost of huge demonstrations and strikes. Agreements with the International Atomic Energy Agency and with the United States would

[2] The "analysts" referred to by Dr. Osgood in his essay.

have to be revised or broken. Nuclear fuel would have to be imported with no strings attached. A testing site would have to be found. It is questionable whether enough Japanese scientists, who incline to the left, could be induced to cooperate. The expense, while not prohibitive, might run by one current Japanese estimate to $300–500 million a year for twenty years, and even then the nuclear force would be equal only to that of England or France. Against whom would it be used, and how? And would it not revive fear and suspicion of Japan without adding to Japan's actual ability to influence events in Asia?

And so while the nuclear-shy Japanese are having their first open debate on these questions, the fact is that government leaders have concluded that the time is not ripe to start producing nuclear weapons. The most positive of them ask only that the options be kept open, and this of course is being done: Japan is moving forward rapidly in the development of nuclear power and rocketry; in fifteen years it may be the world's leading producer of nuclear energy for peaceful uses. It is estimated that if and when Japan decides to become a nuclear power, weapons could be produced in about two years. Meanwhile, the defense budget remains at the relatively low figure of 1.1 percent of gross national product, and this percentage is not expected to rise much during the current defense plan (1967–71).

Without its own nuclear force, and with Communist China building a strategic force of its own, the government continues to believe that the only practical alternative is the security treaty with the United States and the American nuclear umbrella. A sudden withdrawal by the United States from the Pacific or a serious threat from China could change these calculations, but at the moment most conservative leaders favor continuing the treaty after 1970, when it can be legally terminated on one year's notice; even left-wing leaders doubt that the riots of 1960 will be repeated.

The government, however, is as usual out ahead of the public in its support of the treaty. A poll taken in 1967 shows that only 37.7 percent of the people actually support the treaty, 13.9 percent are opposed, 18.2 percent consider it unavoidable, 7.9 percent have other opinions, and 23.1 percent don't know. Despite Diet ratification of the revised treaty in 1960, there is still a feeling among many Japanese that the treaty serves American interests more than their own. Far from being seen as a munificent gift from Washington in return for which the Japanese should be happy to play a supporting role, it is at best a burden that defies the new nationalism, and at worst a lightning rod that in a world war might attract a hail of missiles.

In the United States we tend to feel that we should have a voice in Japan's military posture since we provide most of its security; many Japanese feel, rightly or wrongly, that their tolerance of foreign bases and troops in Japan for purposes going beyond the defense of Japan evens the score. Because of these attitudes, the government is severely restricted in its ability to play a more active role within the framework of the current treaty.

It may not, after all, be so important that Washington continues to lecture Japan on the virtues of "defense-mindedness," since the days when we could influence Japan's policies are largely over. It is worth remembering, though, that our involvement in domestic issues has brought some unexpected results. Consider, for example, the fact that the United States was instrumental in setting up Sohyo, the huge (4.5 million) labor federation, which promptly became the leading opponent of the security treaty and has fought it ever since. There is, of course, a fine irony in the fact that by urging Japan to rearm ever since 1950 we have unwittingly thrown the weight of nationalist sentiment to the side of holding down the size of the army. And there is irony, too, in the fact that those in the Pentagon who have led the drive to induce Japan to rearm will be the first to shout betrayal should Japan use its new arms to pursue independent or competitive objectives.

It would be well if all parts of the American government could find common answers to two questions: First, how do we want to see Japan's new power used in the future? And second, to what extent, if any, can we influence the directions it will take?

If my assessment of the direction of popular attitudes and political trends is correct, it is inconceivable that Japan will agree in the coming decade to associate itself more closely with our strategic objective of containing Communist China. And as the desire to get out from under the American shadow grows, as it surely will, Japan will be even less content with a subordinate role. Fields other than conventional military power, such as space, technology and economic prosperity will be found to satisfy the need for international prestige.

It may be that by asking for less, we will gain more. It could be that after Vietnam, we will redefine our own concept of power in Asia, relying less on conventional military force and more on economic development to deal with the predictable

insurgencies of the future. In such an event, and as-
suming that Communist China continues to be contained by our nuclear deterrent and the Seventh
Fleet, a stable, wealthy, and independent Japan
could be more valuable to us than a closely allied
and more heavily armed Japan. It could be a mag-
netic attraction as Asia's first and most successful
open society, in stark contrast to the dreary alternative of communism on the mainland. Its very lack
of offensive military power might actually make it
a more trusted source of capital and technology. Its
own experience in rapid modernization in an Asian
setting, its relevant agricultural experience and its
racial affinity would all add to its influence.

Finally, a Japan that is not closely tied to our military containment strategy might in the long run
prove to be the link by which the Chinese return to
the real world. Already Peking is looking to Japan
for technology, and if it is true that a developing
China is less dangerous to world peace than a hun-
gry and frustrated China, Japan might serve as a useful bridge. Once before, at the turn of the century,
Japan briefly played a similar role, educating a generation of Chinese leaders in western technology; a
more rational regime in Peking might turn again toward Tokyo for assistance. While all this is speculation, it is interesting to note that even in the current
furor of the Cultural Revolution, conservative Japanese leaders are thinking along these lines. Despite
our efforts to make them fear Peking, most Japanese
believe that their long-range interests will be better
served by building closer ties to the mainland and
by trying to moderate China's current militancy.

Our special relationship with Japan will survive
the war in Vietnam and could ultimately be the

basis for peace in Asia. But it is going to take hard work on both sides, and out of habit and frustration we will continue to advise the Japanese on defense and security problems. Whether we are right or wrong may not matter very much, because they will make the decisions. But it is worth considering the possibility that, in holding down their defense expenditures, avoiding becoming a dependent junior partner in American military strategy, and keeping a door open to China, they may be on the right track.

III. JAPAN'S NONMILITARY ROAD TO POWER

by John H. Badgley

Japan is gradually resuming the stature of an active great power in Asia. Cautiously but persistently, it is taking on a larger role that will express more independently the nation's interests in security and status and yet remain acceptable—in Japan and outside—in view of the political and psychological constraints upon Japan's resurgence as a regional power.

Japan is seeking this larger role not through the traditional methods of a great military power but by supporting economic development in the Asian-Pacific region, and particularly in Southeast Asia. Its regional development program may lead Japan toward growing concern for Asian security problems and efforts to meet them by technical and military assistance to Southeast Asian states, but Japan's expanding role neither requires nor is likely to result in a direct military presence like the United States has established in the area.

Japan's emergence as an active Asian power can best be understood as a product of the fusion of historical tendencies, postwar policies, and present economic, political, and military realities. In this es-

The author wishes to express his appreciation for the time and resources provided by members of the staffs of the Defense Services Historical Institute, Rangoon; Chulalongkorn University, Bangkok; and Kyoto University. Professors Masamichi Inoki, Masataka Kosaka, and Yoshitaro Katsuda reviewed an earlier draft of this essay.

48

say I will describe briefly the causes and character-istics of Japan's regional activity and suggest how the present embryonic trends may and, I believe, should evolve.

Japan's foreign policy since World War II has been shaped by two central considerations: the special relationship with the United States and the quest for an increasing share of world trade. The need for a secure trade pattern dates from the 1920s. Its importance was demonstrated by Japan's willing-ness to go to war with the United States because of a trade embargo and the prospect of losing oil ship-ments from Southeast Asia. The postwar alliance with the United States was a new experience for Ja-pan and led to a fundamental disruption of Japan's classical cultural union with northeast Asia. The al-liance demonstrated the power of advanced military and economic technology to overcome the formerly decisive effect of Japan's proximity to the Asian mainland on its foreign relations.

A third important feature of Japan's foreign policy since World War II has been its profound antimili-tarism. This is reflected, for example, in Japan's com-mitment to the United Nations, which entails legal and diplomatic support but excludes the contribu-tion of military forces. The government's reluctance to amend constitutional provisions outlawing all but defensive forces (thus far interpreted as preventing Japanese troops from serving with the United Na-tions) when Premier Sato raised the issue of new defense requirements is testimony to the ebbing but still powerful pacifist sentiment in Japan.

But although the central characteristics of Ja-panese foreign policy remain constant, economic and social movements within Japan are eroding political support for them. Rapid economic growth, which has made Japan more productive and more dependent on a free world market than the United Kingdom, has also created severe internal tension. For a minority of undetermined size, greater affluence has contributed to a sense of increased national power and a demand for a more independent foreign policy. The business and political leaders with a "capitalist," free-world orientation, who have controlled foreign and domestic policy, are now opposed by this group. Many of the dissenters seek not only termination of the American alliance but also re-identification with Asia, believing that Japan's future, like her prewar past, is inextricably bound to Asia and particularly to China. China's communism (except for the Cultural Revolution) appeals ideologically to Socialists, who retain about a third of the vote; racial and cultural affinity with China, as well as guilt over the destructiveness of the war, lead many non-Socialist intellectuals, conservative Liberal Democrats, and Soka Gakkai's Komei Party members to look toward the mainland; and some sectors of the business community hope that China will again become a major market. These dissenting groups feel that Japan must somehow re-engage with Asia, accommodate China, and return to an independent, nonaligned foreign policy.[1] General concern about American policy toward China and Vietnam, and fear of being drawn into a war not of

[1] For a concise review in English of dissenting views, see essays by Shinkichi Eto, Shuichi Kato, Hajime Terasawa, and Shintaro Ryu in *Journal of Social and Political Ideas in Japan*, Vol. IV, No. 1, April 1966. See also Douglas Mendel, "Japanese Views of Sato's Foreign Policy," *Asian Survey*, Vol. VII, No. 7, July 1967, pp. 444–56.

Japan's choosing, accentuate the opposition of these groups to the government.

In response, the government seems to be developing a new principle in foreign policy, one that might accommodate the free-world orientation, dominant for the past two decades, and the Asian orientation, held both by those with progressive ideological beliefs and by those with conservative cultural attachments. This principle is "regional development." It proposes that Japan play a major role in political and economic affairs among states of the Pacific basin and in Southeast Asia. Specifically, the five advanced states—Japan, the United States, Canada, New Zealand, and Australia—and the rapidly developing states—South Korea, Taiwan, Malaysia, Singapore, Thailand, and the Philippines—seem to fall within this regional view.[2] Such a policy would bring into question the view that has prevailed in Japan since World War II: that it should not play a major political role in world affairs. But regional development may secure support from those who are eager to see Japan play a more independent role in Asian affairs, and especially from businessmen who want assurance that their foreign investments will be protected and profitable.

[2] The first concrete application of this principle was Japan's decision of 1966 to join the Asian and Pacific Council. In 1967 the joint communiqué of the United States-Japan Committee on Trade and Economic Affairs, Part IV, emphasized the same regional development principle. Statements by Premier Sato on visits to Southeast Asian States (September 1967) and the United States (November 1967), commitments to the Asian Development Bank, Australia, South Korea, Malaysia, the Philippines, Taiwan, and Thailand, and diplomatic support for the Association of Southeast Asian Nations, give credence to the idea.

The new orientation that Japan's policies may acquire could provide economic benefits, especially if it were to proscribe an anticommunist position with a view to greater trade and investment in China. It would also allow broad cooperation with the other major states in Asia—India, Pakistan, and Indonesia—all of which seek closer economic relations with Japan in order to bolster their development programs. However, the politically hostile leadership in China and the monumental problems facing all four of these major underdeveloped states have limited the interest of Japanese businessmen and of the government in investments or large-scale assistance. Of the four states, only Indonesia has attracted new capital in significant amounts from Japan in the past two years.

Although economic considerations currently provide the chief incentive for Japanese activity in the Asian-Pacific region, concern for political influence and security will probably grow, especially in regard to Southeast Asia. The basis for this speculation is threefold. First, there is a historic precedent for Japanese political involvement in regional affairs. Second, trade interests and heavy commitments to economic development usually arouse political interest, as with the French in their former African colonies, the United States in India and Pakistan, and the Soviet Union in the Middle East. This process seems to be at work already in Japan's relations with Taiwan, Korea, and several Southeast Asian states, and is accelerated by a special interest in trying to prevent hostile groups from gaining power in these countries. Third, many Japanese would like to see their country act as a buffer—albeit a non-nuclear buffer—between the United States and China in order to reduce the possibility of nuclear war.

These three factors in themselves do not necessarily dictate a greater political role for Japan in Asia. Moreover, Japanese political activity may be constrained by Japan's efforts to seek free access to world trade and to maintain a special relationship with the United States, insofar as these traditional objectives persist. Nevertheless, it seems reasonable to assume that Japan's deep-rooted interest in status, trade, and peace will eventually lead her to acquire larger political interests and responsibilities, especially in Southeast Asia. At the same time, the evidence also suggests that, despite its expanding role, Japan will probably retain its defensive, non-expansionist military posture—that, in effect, it has learned its lesson from World War II.

The roots of Japan's re-emergence as an active major power in Asia lie partly in the historical tendency of Japan to seek and, with some notable reversals, attain influence and status in Southeast Asia. The premodern pattern of Japanese foreign relations was based mainly on trade, concern for security, and respect for China's culture and power. Japan also attempted to claim suzerainty over various parts of eastern Asia and occasionally went to war in support of its claims between the thirteenth and seventeenth centuries. But at the beginning of the seventeenth century, after many years of internal disorder, Japan closed itself off from the rest of the world in order to secure its immediate island empire, and efforts to establish control elsewhere were allowed to lapse for three centuries.

By the late nineteenth century, Japan had acquired such a strong sense of cultural unity and nationhood that it was able to modernize and establish itself as a major power within a short period of time. As its energies turned outward again, its technological and military strength won admiration in many parts of Asia, especially where Japanese economic expansion and large-scale migration occurred But Asian peoples also feared that Japan's power might eventually be directed against them. When Japan's efforts to establish political and often military control in the wake of its economic expansion met disaster at the end of World War II, Japan was forced to realize that nationalist movements were determined to resist such control and that greater racial affinity and anticolonialism alone could not make Japan welcome in Southeast Asia.

The experience of the war, and Japan's domestic reaction to it, brought about not an end to Japanese-Asian relations but rather a new phase, characterized by the gradual re-establishment of normal trade relations and substantial reparations payments. The government sought markets in the Asian-Pacific region as in the rest of the world. By 1948, trade had climbed out of the postwar trough: rice, rubber, copra, oil, sisal, and metal ores were imported by Japan and manufactured goods reappeared on Asian markets. Reparations aid began to flow in 1955, and the reparations agreements had guaranteed by 1966 $2.3 billion worth of technical aid and capital to Burma, Indonesia, the Philippines, the Indochina states, and Korea. About $50 million was allocated annually after 1955, in addition to which Japanese private capital was invested in substantial amounts after 1960 in Thailand, Malaysia, and the Philippines. In 1965, after fourteen years of negotiations, Korea also signed a reparations treaty for a half-billion dollars in grants and loans to be paid over a twenty-year period.

Thus, before and since World War II, Japan's regional economic interests have been extensive enough to promise that Japan will continue to play a large and increasing economic role in the Asian-Pacific area. That Japan's economic involvement may well lead to expanded political influence and activity, as in the past, is indicated by Japan's decision in 1966 to join the Asian and Pacific Council. However, the fact that Japan's increasing regional economic and political activity has since the war been accompanied by persistent self-restraint in military matters, indeed by persistent pacifism, suggests that Japan's military role may well remain less vital than that of the United States in East and Southeast Asia in the forseeable future. Japan's cautious military policy, in turn, promotes its growing economic role by making the accompanying political influence acceptable.

Another factor that creates favorable attitudes toward Japan's regional activity, both within the country and among the underdeveloped states in Asia, is Japan's achievement of modern success in a uniquely Asian form. Many Japanese take great pride in having preserved their historical and cultural individuality while successfully acquiring modern western technology, and feel a sense of obligation toward other Asians who seek to develop themselves without destroying their historical identities. This sentiment creates a favorable domestic climate for programs of regional development assistance.

In the poorer Asian states outside Japan, government elites must increase the state's political power as rapidly as possible in order to survive. Modernization is the key to such power. Government leaders confront a psychological dilemma because the source of modernity is the West, yet these leaders have often gained power through their successful opposition to western colonial rule, and they continue to resist western cultural influence. The "true" Burmese, Indonesian, or Cambodian, like the "true" Japanese, must demonstrate belief in his "national" tradition or lose the faith of fellow patriots. But, because there is confusion over the meaning of nationalism in new states everywhere, antiwestern sentiment has served as a functional substitute while a new positive tradition is gradually defined. Thus, to draw on western achievements in the effort to develop threatens their identity as nationals. In particular, those leaders who are nursing an embryonic national culture seek to blunt the influence of the United States, the most powerful western state and the symbolic spearhead of the West's cultural offensive. Japan shares with the weaker Asian states a concern for national integrity in the face of western influence, and thus represents the possibility of achieving modernity in a uniquely Asian mode. Although most Asian states are distinguished from Japan by endemic internal conflict and political weakness and by racial and cultural heterogeneity, which prevents Japan's development experience from being entirely transferable, the Japanese development model nonetheless demonstrates the conditions for successful Asian modernization: cultural consolidation, savings and capital accumulation, educational and administrative resources, and political stability.

Although Japan's ability to play a leading role in Southeast Asian affairs rests on its demonstration of successful modernization as an Asian state, the country's influence over its neighbors will flow from the most dramatic outward manifestation of that success: its economic power and interests and the reciprocity these activities have created and will foster among its trading partners. At the end of World War II Japan's relations with its neighbors had collapsed, but after a relatively short hiatus it was possible to rebuild normal trade relations and establish a peacetime policy based on economic

TABLE ONE[3]

Trade with Southeast Asia
(includes India and Pakistan)

Imports (%)		Exports (%)
16.8	1936	15.6
20.3	1956	26.6
16.1	1958	23.1
18.0	1960	24.9
14.8	1962	21.8
14.8	1963	22.1

TABLE TWO[4]

Credit Commitments by Area
(includes top 85%)   (in millions of yen)

	Fiscal 1965		Fiscal 1966	
Southeast Asia	54,918	27%	65,548	23%
Europe	55,930	27	66,329	23
Africa	37,190	18	71,895	25
East Asia	25,372	12	31,252	11

[3] From Leon Hollerman, *Japan's Dependence on the World Economy* (Princeton: Princeton University Press, 1967), p. 98.

[4] From the Export-Import Bank of Japan, *Annual Report, 1967*, p. 6. The sharp rise in African credits between 1965 and 1966 reflected a heavy commitment to the South African automobile industry. Investment in Southeast Asia for the period rose over 10 billion yen.

activity. By 1965 Japan had become a major trade partner with Australia, New Zealand, the Philippines, Taiwan, Thailand, Malaysia, Singapore, Indonesia, and most of its other neighbors; and trade is the major avenue through which Japan currently influences development planning in Southeast Asia. Japan ranks first or second as exporter to most Southeast Asian countries, imports about a fifth of the region's exports, and is expected to become increasingly important as a supplier in the 1970s and 1980s.[5] Because Southeast Asian countries export mostly primary products and foods (which are subject to sharp fluctuations on the world market, steadily declining terms of trade, and restrictive EEC tariffs), they face severe difficulties in bridging the gap between the value of their exports and the cost of their imports. Japan's trade practices have, in effect, guaranteed some commodity purchases (e.g., tin, iron ore, rubber) and prices, thereby subsidizing necessary imports for its trading partners in the region. Such a policy increases Japan's political leverage, or at least the potential for it, because Southeast Asian states, like nearly all underdeveloped states, are dependent on hard currency loans to purchase capital goods. An assured market, even though it is partial, is therefore extremely important for these states, who become to some degree dependent upon Japan for it. Yen credits granted through the Export-Import bank for private investors and reparations negotiated through the Ministry for International Trade and Investment (MITI) are other sources of Japanese influence. The system transfers capital and skills, and local firms thereby

[5] See the ECAFE study in *Economic Bulletin for Asia and the Far East*, Vol. XIV, No. 3, December 1963.

learn to produce import substitutes, for MITI encourages development of labor intensive industries, such as cotton textile manufacturing, which displaces inefficient Japanese manufacturers.

Such policies gain influence for Japan in development planning, and indirectly over some political decisions by rewarding "sound" politics and withholding funds from regimes that would create disequilibrium in Southeast Asia. Most illustrative of this spillover effect between economics and politics is the Indonesian case. During the last three years of Sukarno's administration, Japanese credits, except for reparations, were quite skimpy. After 1966 several hundred firms sent representatives to Indonesia; nearly $300 million worth of investment has been promised since, and Japanese banks began granting lower interest rates on loans as well as longer-term loans. Examples of long-range investment range from the largest foreign commitment in 1967, the $200 million Lampung rice project in South Sumatra (a cooperative venture of combined Japanese and Indonesian firms), to nonferrous metals, petroleum exploration franchises and new banking guarantees.

Japan is in a particularly good position to assist Southeast Asian development, not only because it is the nearest industrial market but also because it has attained very high efficiency and productivity in a number of fields especially important for development. Its technical competence and managerial organization in electronics, chemicals, steel, vehicles, and ship building are excellent. Japan is also more competitive than other industrial states in providing machinery and chemical products.

As the most powerful modern state in Asia except for the Soviet Union, Japan can provide large investments for development. After 1960, its investments climbed sharply in the whole Asian-Pacific area; since 1965, the amount invested in Southeast Asia has risen precipitously and constitutes a quarter of Japan's total overseas commitments in the current decade. These investments have created a broad demand for skilled manpower in Southeast Asia, and Japanse corporate training programs for Southeast Asians are responding to this need by educating such diverse groups as bankers, auto and electronic repairmen, plant foremen, fishery and cold storage specialists, and even cinematographers.

In addition to trade exchanges and investments, Japan gains influence through the Asian Development Bank, which it has joined as an equal contributor with the United States. The Bank was established with thirty-one members in 1966. The same year, at Korea's instigation, the Asian and Pacific Council was organized to advance "regional security." Its membership included Japan, Australia, New Zealand, the Philippines, Malaysia, Singapore, Thailand, South Vietnam, and South Korea. These commitments have involved no major political obligations, yet they indicate a new quality in Japan's understanding of the role it ought to play in Southeast Asia.

If Japan's regional development role is to be expanded, many powerful institutions in Japan—agriculture, industry, commerce, government bureaucracies, mass media, political parties, and the universities—must be involved. The several media forms, particularly television and journalism, have helped awaken the Japanese public to conditions of poverty as well as cultural distinctiveness in the rest of Asia. In the public sector, Japan initiated annual Southeast Asian ministerial conferences on agricultural and industrial development problems in 1966. However, the Foreign, Finance, Trade, and Industries Ministries, all concerned with foreign assistance, have often been at odds in their Asian policies. The Finance Ministry is very cautious in accepting new commitments, whereas the Foreign Ministry and the Ministry for International Trade and Investment frequently push for a greater political role.

The commercial community's contacts in Southeast Asia through joint cooperatives and in civic clubs—such as the influential Rotary organizations in Taipei, Bangkok, and Manila—provide an institutionalized means of extending personal relationships among business elites. Private agricultural experts, particularly forestry and rice specialists, are recruited by the Agriculture Ministry for United Nations agencies and regional groups such as ECAFE and the Colombo plan, as well as by direct hire as in the Lampung project.

The most widespread interest in regional development and modernization is found in the universities, where research has led to much more sophisticated knowledge about regional problems. More research on Southeast Asia, in both the social and natural sciences, is now being conducted in Japan than in any other country outside the United States.

Japan's future influence upon her Asian neighbors will depend largely on persuasive communication of intentions and closer cultural relations. Language is central to communications requirements. The Japanese have a disability compared to the Americans and other English speakers because English is the second language for most of the region's educated population. Some Japanese working in Asian countries have command of the national language—Thai, Korean, Burmese, Tagalog, Indonesian, or Khmer—but, since most Japanese work only a short period in a country, English is usually used. The Japanese enjoy some advantage over other non-English speaking peoples because of the widespread use of English since the American occupation.

Of greater importance is the cultural activity being conducted in many Asian states by both public and private Japanese institutions. Among foreign imports, Japanese films are second only to American ones in popularity in Southeast Asia. Their overseas programming, television, movies, and magazines are increasingly available in local languages. Lectures, performing tours by artists, trade fairs, scholarships, and trainee programs are all aspects of the cultural affairs program.

Despite the lack of a domestic consensus about foreign policy, a broad view of Japanese activities in many fields suggests that Japan will become increasingly involved in Southeast Asia and that its involvement will generate growing Japanese influence.

China is now the primary threat to Japan's security. However, to some Japanese this threat seems to be accentuated by the American military presence in Southeast Asia. They argue that active military intervention of the most powerful country in the world provokes Chinese efforts to counter that presence in Southeast Asia. Moreover, American intervention, as the intrusion of a western power into

Asia gives rise to nationalistic movements in Southeast Asia, which the Chinese can make use of to resist American activity. If this American role were superseded by an expanded economic and political role of Japan, which is weaker and less racially intrusive, China might be deprived of these causes and opportunities for expansionist policies in Southeast Asia. China is too weak and preoccupied with domestic difficulties to be a serious military threat to the area. So goes the argument by those Japanese who oppose a continued American military presence in Southeast Asia.

They reason that the American involvement in Vietnam and the sharp Sino-American conflict it creates give rise to a particular danger for Japan and they fear that the conflict may erupt in nuclear war causing Japan, because of its American alliance, to fall victim to China's nuclear force in such a war. This danger is the basis of opposition leftist and Komeito criticism of Japan's defense policies. It has persuaded many Japanese that Sino-American tensions must be relieved by removing or at least diminishing the root cause, the American presence near China's borders. This might be accomplished by a settlement in Southeast Asia—perhaps neutralization—that would evict the United States, and by the expansion of Japanese activities in Southeast Asia to create a buffer of Japanese influence between Chinese and American interest. Without a major American presence in Southeast Asia, Japanese development aid and military assistance may well create stability in the area and yet avoid posing a threat to China, which would then have little reason or encouragement to endanger Southeast Asian states and Japanese interests there.

This view is open to criticism by the arguments that development and military aid do not necessarily create stability and that, despite either diminished American provocation or stability under Japan's aegis, China seeks to disrupt existing politics and acquire hegemony in Southeast Asia. Moreover, some governments in the region seek military support in order to counter Chinese-supported incursions and to secure a monopoly of violence against general domestic insurgency: for them American military assistance has been the most dependable in provision and maintenence.

Nevertheless, in the next ten years, Japan will probably improve the technical and organizational quality of its military forces with new aircraft and new communications systems to suit a new generation of missile armaments, new forms of transport, especially helicopters and troop carriers, and new naval craft to improve the defensive capability of Japan's large marine and fishing fleet. Japan would therefore be in a position to supply some military aid to Southeast Asia, and will have an increasing incentive for doing so if its economic and political involvement there expands. This aid might eventually extend to logistical support for Southeast Asian governments in maintaining security, but the mood of the Japanese public is quite unlikely to allow actual intervention of Japanese military forces in Southeast Asia.

The preceding speculations about the extent and nature of Japan's military role in Southeast Asia are relevant only to the reasonably foreseeable future, or about the next decade. One cannot sensibly speculate about the form that Japan's military involvement may take after that time. Pressures from China, encouragement from Southeast Asian leaders, and arguments by security-conscious leaders in Japan might conceivably lead Japan to undertake an actively interventionist role in Southeast Asia in the 1980s or afterward. The reassertion of Japanese influence in the region might even create pressures for Japanese nuclear weapons as a counter to the Chinese nuclear force, as the present constraints on Japan's acquiring such weapons dissolved. But at this time one can only surmise that whether or not Japan's expanding economic and political activity in Southeast Asia leads to a military role comparable to the American presence there may depend largely on whether Japan develops policies of economic and military assistance that create general stability in the region, and whether, in turn, Chinese policies are moderated by this achievement. If these conditions prevail, Japan may once more assume the role of a major participant in the Asian balance of power —only this time it would be as a stabilizing economic power with a nonmilitary role.